Thriving Beyond the Margins

GUY HAMMOND

Thriving Beyond the Margins

How the Same-Sex Attracted CAN Live Faithful Christian Lives

*A Six-Part Bible Study Workbook
for Friends Helping Friends*

ILLUMINATION PUBLISHERS

Thriving Beyond the Margins

ISBN: 978-1-939086-87-7. Printed in the United States of America.

Unless otherwise noted, all Scripture quotations are taken from the *Holy Bible*, New International Version, copyright ©1973, 1978, 1984, 2011 by Biblica, Inc. Used by permission. All rights reserved worldwide.

Scriptures marked NLT are from the *Holy Bible, New Living Translation* copyright © 1996, 2004, 2007 by Tyndale House Foundation. Used by permission of Tyndale House Publishers Inc., Carol Stream, Illinois 60188. All rights reserved.

Scripture references marked NKJV are from *The Holy Bible, New King James Version*®. Copyright © 1982 by Thomas Nelson, Inc. All rights reserved.

Cover and interior book design: Toney C. Mulhollan.

Illumination Publishers cares deeply about the environment and uses recycled paper whenever possible.

About the author: Before becoming a Christian in 1987, Guy Hammond lived an active homosexual lifestyle for fourteen years, two years of which were spent in the gay community of Toronto, Canada. Upon his conversion to Jesus, Guy left that life behind forever, and although his same-gender attractions have never diminished, he has been determined that his identity be found in Jesus, not in his sexual orientation.

Over the years, God has blessed Guy's life tremendously. He has been married to his wife, Cathy, for twenty-five years, and they have four amazing children. Today Guy is an evangelist, a best-selling author, and professional public speaker. He is the founder and Executive Director of Strength in Weakness Ministries (www.strengthinweakness.org), an organization that provides support to other same-sex attracted Christians, and educates the church on how to successfully share the good news of Christ with those in the GLBTQ (gay, lesbian, bisexual, transgender, queer) communities in a manner that is compassionate, respectful, and consistent with the biblical sexual ethic.

Table of Contents

Before you begin:
Are You Teaching Your Friend About Christ?
(Don't skip over this part . . . seriously.)

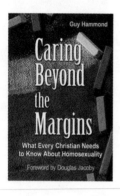

Some insights in these Bible studies come from my book, *Caring Beyond the Margins: What Every Christian Needs to Know About Homosexuality*. It is crucial that you have the right heart and mindset before you begin helping people from the lesbian, gay, bisexual, transgender, queer (LGBTQ) community. Please read these basic insights before you get started.

So you have the opportunity to study the Scriptures with someone who is same-sex attracted, or who identifies themselves as gay, lesbian, bisexual or transgender. Congratulations. What an honor!

Before you begin to speak, please spend time considering these truths. You will need to understand and accept them with your heart, mind and sentiment so that your dialogue can be relevant and "seasoned with salt" (Colossians 4:6):

1. **Every person needs to be treated with dignity, kindness and respect,** regardless of who they are attracted to, how they choose to live their lives, or what they believe regarding

sexual expression and matters of faith.

2. **The issue is about people, not sexual orientation.** As we read in *Sexual Identity: A Guide to Living in the Time Between the Times,*

    "All too often, whenever the church talks about homosexuality, it is in the context of something to oppose, but when the church talks about homosexuality it should be talked about in the context of people.... We need to see beyond gay, see beyond lesbian and see a person. We can act or come across, whether we intend to or not, as though sex or sexual attraction is the only defining factor in a human being. It is an important factor, but it's not someone's whole identity.... Many Christians think they do not have any close personal relationships with gay people and their perspectives and attitudes have been influenced by an interpersonal experience; things they've read or heard, or seen on television, or on the news. But behind the headlines, behind the faces on a screen, are the lives of real men, women and young people who navigate the reality of same-gender attraction in a society that makes it a constant uphill battle. Beyond the land of theoretical rhetoric and arguments and standing one's ground and political battles and choosing sides, lie real people, with real hurts and dreams and talents and families and careers and joys and sorrows and bills and exams and loves and lives."[1]

3. **Many gay and lesbian people do want to know God.** It is a misconception that all homosexuals are uninterested in matters of faith and the Bible.

4. **Christians do not have all the answers on this topic.** While God has clearly defined that active homosexuality is sinful, beyond that reality the Bible does not say a lot on this topic besides some indirect references to homosexuality, like the story of Lot (Genesis 19, Jude 7, 2 Peter 2:6–7). The Bible actually only discusses homosexuality directly five times (Leviticus 18:22 and 20:13, Romans 1:26–27, 1 Corinthians 6:9–10 and 1 Timothy 1:9–10), and it certainly does not speak to causation.

   What causes homosexuality? The truth is, no one knows for sure. There are many contributing influences as to why someone is homosexually attracted, and neither the Bible nor science has given any definitive answers in this regard. About the only thing we know for sure is that no one chooses to be homosexually attracted. As with everyone, people who are same-gender attracted certainly do choose what they will do with their attraction, but the attraction itself is mostly automatic and involuntary.

   Because this topic is so complex, I suggest you speak with hesitancy when addressing this issue. This means that you will need to be honest both when you do have an answer, and when you do not. It means that you will need to be comfortable with the fact that much surrounding this topic is ambiguous. It means that when you teach the biblical sexual ethic, you must do it boldly, yes—but also with compassion, sensitivity, kindness, and—most importantly—with humility.

5. **Same-sex attraction is not the first issue you should address.** For some reason, we often seem to think that when we are talking to a same-sex attracted individual about God, the first thing we need to tackle is their sexual orientation. Why? There is a whole person there that will need to be transformed into the likeness of Christ. This will be a process that will take time as the Holy Spirit moves in this person's life to bring them to conviction.

    Surely there must be other topics and issues you can cover and teach besides their sexual attractions! Of course you will eventually get to what the Bible teaches regarding sex and relationships, but to go after their sexuality as a first priority and to allow that issue to dominate the discussion would mean that your priorities are out of whack and that you are not seeing the big picture in this person's life or God's will for them.

6. **Let me relieve you of the pressure of having all of the answers on the issues of sexual identity and homosexuality.** This is a complex, multi-faceted subject; no one has all the answers. Sometimes we have to be happy to live in the land of "I don't know." And know this: the person with whom

you are studying won't expect you to have all the answers. What will impress them more than anything else will be your honesty, kindness, hospitality, and the fact that you genuinely care for them.

7. **My final word of advice is this: do not make promises you cannot keep.** Don't tell people that their attractions to the same gender will leave them if they become a Christian or get married. Don't offer simple (and sometimes offensive) antidotes like "play more sports" or "go on more dates with the opposite sex" or "just have more faith" or "pray harder." While God is certainly able to transform anyone he chooses in whatever fashion he desires, he often chooses not to. In fact, God loves to use the vulnerable, weaker areas of our lives for us to glorify him in helping others. The reality is, having a heterosexual orientation is not a prerequisite for being a follower of Jesus and being saved. There are many, many disciples who are same-sex attracted and yet are living faithful lives to the Lord and glorifying him with their lives. The goal is not that people become heterosexually attracted; the goal is that they live holy lives. Let me repeat that: *The goal is not that people become heterosexually attracted; the goal is that they live holy lives.*

If you can converse with these things in mind, you'll have a great head start in being able to speak the truth in love.

Are You Teaching Your Friend About Christ?
How Best to Use These Studies
(And don't skip this part, either!)

This series is not a replacement for whatever Bible study series, classes or protocol that your local church usually uses in bringing people to Christ; rather, it is an additional set of studies to be used *in conjunction with* the Bible study series that you would use with anyone when teaching them about Christ.

When teaching our friends and neighbors about Christ, there are many different methods and formats that can be followed. Is one better than another? I don't know. It probably has more to do with what you, as the instructor and guide of the studies, feel most comfortable with. That being said, I would like to suggest a method that may be somewhat unorthodox, but is one I think best, considering the subject matter.

First, I suggest that you and your friend read through each study together, like you would an article or chapter in a book, and then discuss it together. The studies are authored in a conversational tone. You won't find a list of scriptures, followed by a discussion for each passage, but rather a Bible study that is written more like a chapter in a book. Don't worry, the scriptures are there, but I fill in the gaps between the scriptures sharing from my years of experience as a man who was converted from a homosexual life and has lived for almost three decades as a same-sex attracted follower of Jesus. The idea is that you read each study together, from beginning to end (this will take about twenty minutes), and then discuss.

SOME FINAL POINTERS

- Don't start these Bible studies until you and the person you are helping have agreed that the Scriptures are the authoritative word of God. I would suggest beginning your Bible studies with a study about God's word. If a person does not accept the authority of the Bible, then they will have a difficult time moving forward with further study. If you are studying with a person who has been entrenched in the gay community for many years, it might also be wise to wait to introduce these studies after you have completed a study on the cross of Christ. People must be moved by the death of Jesus in order to be willing to make the complete lifestyle change that is necessary to be a disciple of Christ.

- Do this series in the order that it is presented here. The studies were arranged in a particular order for a reason, so please respect that (although it is fine to intersperse these studies with the primary study series you are using).

- Take your time. It's not a race. Doing one study a week or even every few weeks is fine. Don't rush people. Remember, be patient, hospitable and loving, and keep the dialogue going between the studies.

- The Strength in Weakness Ministry is here to help. Please refer people to our website, **www.strengthinweakness.org**.

- If the person you are assisting becomes a disciple, they are welcome to join our ministry. There is a nominal fee for this, but there they will find Bible studies (Quiet Times), articles, powerful testimonials, and many other helps to assist same-sex attracted disciples. Christian men and women of all ages from all over the world belong to this ministry.

Are You Gay and Looking
for Biblical Answers?
(This note is from me to you.)

I can't begin to tell you how thrilled I am that you have decided to sit down and examine how the Bible and Christianity relate to your life in all areas, but also specifically in the area of sexual purity and homosexuality. It's a courageous step on your part, so I congratulate you.

Of course, while I and the person with whom you are studying the Bible will do our best, we won't be able to answer every question you have. I have questions myself that remain unanswered, and I have had to be willing to live in the tension of uncertainty on some issues of sexual identity and attraction. The topic is complex, for sure. But I do hope that these studies will propel honest conversation with open Bibles and open hearts.

Why did I write this series of studies? Before I became a Christian at the age of 26, I had lived an active homosexual life for almost 14 years. I had a boyfriend for almost 10 years, and in the final 24 months before I became a Christian, I had gay sex with multiple partners as I lived out my gay life in Toronto.

I spent more than a decade participating in homosexual activity. During that time I engaged in clandestine and anonymous sexual encounters with strangers, lived a double life, hid in plain sight, was dishonest about my homosexuality with people I was close to, and lived in constant fear that I would hurt people if they knew the truth about me. Add to that a broken relationship with a boyfriend of several years, and by 1987, I found myself unhappy and unfulfilled. My lifestyle had taken a terrible toll.

During this time I was invited to attend a church service that deeply impressed me. I was open to going to church because the many contradictions in my life had left me unhappy and confused. I was searching for answers.

It took some time for me to build trust with the Christians, but in them I saw and experienced a love, kindness and hospitality that I had never seen before. Of course the Bible moved my heart, too, because I just couldn't get over the fact that Jesus would die for me.

After much thought and soul-searching, I finally became a Christian, and left my active gay life behind forever. I say "active" because while I have not participated in any kind of homosexual activity since my conversion in 1987, I am still same-sex attracted. (We will discuss how that works in a future study.)

I will admit that for a period of years, I found homosexuality exciting, fun, and even satisfying. Homosexuality worked for me in a lot of ways, as I'm sure it has for you. The truth is, I didn't leave homosexuality because I believed at the time that it was so awful; I left homosexuality because I found something better. As beneficial as homosexuality seemed to me at the time,

I became convinced that Jesus could meet my emotional, relational, and spiritual deficits in a way that homosexuality never could. Indeed, Jesus could meet my needs better than *anything else* ever could. Twenty-eight years of Christianity have proven that to be true time and again. Besides this, there is something that Jesus was able to do for me that homosexuality never possibly could, and that is to provide forgiveness of my sins, receive the gift of the Holy Spirit to live inside of me, and give me the promise of heaven in the life hereafter. I figured that's a pretty good deal! People often comment that if a homosexual is genuinely happy in his or her life, then why would a change be necessary? What compelling argument is there for Christianity that someone would be willing to make such a drastic lifestyle change? Well, it's true. Not all gay people are miserable; many have very satisfying and loving relationships with those of the same gender. I can't argue this fact. But regardless how happy and satisfying homosexuality is for many, salvation will never be found there. This fact alone became the primary motivation for me to choose a relationship with Christ over living an active homosexual life.

I hope that as we go through these few studies together, you will begin to discover, as I did, just how amazing Jesus is! I know that even the thought of giving up your homosexual life to become a Christian seems overwhelming to you right now. I want you to know that if you eventually decide to make this move, Jesus will not disappoint you. He will be totally worth it.

STUDY ONE

Celebrating the Freedom of Choice

Scriptures used in this study:

Ecclesiastes 2:1–11

Ecclesiastes 12:13–14

1 Corinthians 5:12

Titus 2:11–14

Deuteronomy 30:11–20

God is such a gentleman. His desire for each one of us is that we accept his invitation to follow him, but it's not his desire that we do so because we are forced. He's too respectful of you and me to do such a thing. He offered up his own son as a sacrifice, and through Jesus, we have the opportunity to receive the forgiveness of our sins. The choice of whether or not we actually become a Christian has been entirely left up to each one of us. God allows us—*wants us*—to decide for ourselves. He does not want to hold us hostage, nor does he want us to act like robots; rather, he gives us free will to choose what we will do with our minds and bodies. This freedom to decide how we will live our lives is a wonderful gift, and whether or not we choose to make the necessary changes to become a

Christian will not affect how much God loves us, for his kind of love is incalculable and unending. Our decision will have a lot to do with whether or not *we are willing* to be a disciple of Jesus.

I'll never forget when I had to make my own decision. I had to choose between the life of homosexuality that I was familiar with, even comfortable with, a life that I had spent a lot of time, money and energy on; versus the lifestyle I saw in the Bible. And the Bible made it clear that *active* homosexuality was not a part of God's plan for human sexuality, and could not be a part of my life if I became a Christian (I'll explain how I came to that conclusion later). Upon being confronted with this biblical truth, I didn't think I could stop, and I was afraid. I spent a lot of time thinking and praying about my decision, but finally decided that I could not ignore the sacrifice Jesus had made for me, and that I wanted Christianity more than I wanted homosexuality. I wanted my sins forgiven and the promise of heaven more than the enjoyments of being in a homosexual relationship. In spite of my fears, I found that real freedom came when I made a final decision and said "no" to my life of homosexuality. Making this decision was an instrument of integrity.

It's true that God didn't take away my attractions to the same gender, for I still live with them today even twenty-eight years after becoming a Christian. Instead, God gave me something even better than the elimination of my homosexual temptations and desires: the ability to deny those enticements and to choose God in their place. Let me add here (and again, I will explain further in another study) that Jesus was totally worth it. He has truly been able to fulfill my emotional, relational and spiritual deficits in ways that fourteen years of homosexuality were never able to do, and I am confident of this: God wants to do the same for you!

That is real freedom: the ability to choose. I may not have chosen my sexual orientation, but I sure do have the ability to choose what I am going to do with my mind and my physical body, and I can unequivocally choose what I will cherish in my heart.

I want to pause here to address an important question that I had and that you probably have too. I often wondered why I was attracted to other men. What had I done to set myself up for this? Here is the realization I have come to: *I do not believe that you and I did something, or failed to do something, that led us to have same-gender attractions. I believe that attractions are automatic and involuntary; we have little say over what we find attractive. However, the Bible makes it clear that a person can choose to act or refrain from acting on their attractions.* When I became a Christian, I chose to deny my same-gender attractions in obedience to God and in honor of his Son.

I consider this to be one of the most amazing truths we find in Christianity: God tells us that we can all choose how to live our lives, and through Christ he gives us the strength to carry out our decisions. The follower of Jesus does not have to be a victim to their every thought and temptation, nor do they have to abide by what society tells them is appropriate or acceptable.

Before I found Christ, I was a slave, unable to turn away from homosexuality, mostly because I couldn't find another viable alternative that provided the love, physical affection and emotional intimacy I longed for. I was frustrated with myself because deep down, I knew that my homosexual lifestyle was morally wrong and ultimately unfulfilling. And yet I couldn't say no, but hey, bad love is better than no love at all. I felt trapped. This paralysis, this feeling of enslavement, led me to search for understanding. Why did I keep going down a path that I knew was both wrong *and* was making me unhappy? Why did this lifestyle have such a hold on me? By the time I was 24 years old, I had acted out over 300 times with other men, many times in dangerous situations and of course, while putting my own physical safety and well being in serious jeopardy. Why? At last I came to this realization: I was living a gay lifestyle because I believed I "had to be me." I believed that somehow I would be betraying who I really was if I did not act out on my desires and embrace my homosexuality.

I couldn't help being a person with same-gender attraction. The attraction was there—automatic and involuntary, as I have said. I simply did not have the capability to stop those desires. In this sense *I did not choose homosexuality; homosexuality chose me.* And so I felt that I had no choice: I was attracted to other men, therefore *I had to act* on those desires. I had to live a homosexual lifestyle. It never occurred to me that there might be another way to live my life. It never occurred to me that I could choose to say "no" to my same-gender attractions.

But the Bible told me just that: I had a choice, and there was another way. When I began to consider following Jesus, God presented me with a choice between two distinct lifestyles: homosexuality and Christianity.

I've heard many same–sex attracted individuals say the same thing I used to tell myself: "I must be true to myself. I am who I am—a homosexual." But for the Christian who is same-gender attracted, such an argument loses all steam when we admit that *who we really are is Christians.* That reality trumps everything: race, heritage, language, skin color, social status, education, and sexual orientation! For the disciple of Jesus, Christianity is our nature and we can't truly be at peace and true to ourselves unless we are following God's path for our lives.

Living life with restraint and being able to say "no" is not something that most people get excited about. But there's something to be said for this ability. "No" is a moment of choice. It announces something affirmative about you. And remember, you cannot have genuine freedom of choice without the freedom to refuse. Let me repeat that: *You cannot have freedom of choice without the freedom to refuse.* Once you can refuse and appreciate the value and benefits of doing so, then and only then, do you have true freedom of choice.

Even Tiger Woods now recognizes the importance of saying "no" for the cause of a greater good and peace in one's life. He shared these sentiments at his infamous press conference, apologizing to the world for all of his infidelities. He talked about the path of choosing self-denial through Buddhism. He said, "Buddhism teaches that a craving for things outside ourselves causes an unhappy and pointless search for security. It teaches me to stop following every impulse and to learn restraint. Obviously I lost track of what I was taught." (February 19, 2010)

It is in that same line of reasoning that when I became a Christian, I chose a path of not following every impulse. I chose to learn restraint and boundaries. I decided to live a life of self-denial in regard to my sexual expression—not in the name of Buddhism but in the name of Jesus Christ.

Now I fully recognize that many people celebrate and embrace homosexuality, and do not agree with what the Bible teaches about sexual expression, and I believe that Christians must respect people's freedom to choose as they desire. Everyone should be free to decide their own path and live by the consequences that they choose. Because God is a God who respects your right to choose your own path, he expects Christians to also show the same respect. (Granted, Christians are not often known for doing well in this area, which is wrong.)

Paul says in 1 Corinthians 5:12–13:

> "What business is it of mine to judge those outside the church? Are you not to judge those inside? God will judge those outside."

And so we will not "judge" you if you decide to continue in your homosexual lifestyle. In this sense, we are equal rights proponents. We respect your right (as God does) to choose how you will live. We also hope that pro-gay proponents will respect other people's right to submit their homoerotic attractions to God and live according to the biblical sexual ethic. Those who choose to do so (like me) are motivated by the mercy and grace of God.

That being said, I encourage people to make an educated choice. As a minister I constantly put before people the challenge to educate themselves in regard to God and the Bible, and I try to help facilitate that education. Why? Because I believe that trying to find love, acceptance and lifelong fulfillment in anything other than Jesus—whether it is heterosexual sex, homosexual sex, drugs, alcohol, food, sleep or massive amounts of entertainment or anything else people turn to instead of God— is a poor imitation of the real thing. All these things will leave us feeling unfulfilled and deceived in the end.

Solomon, the wisest and wealthiest man alive in his time, said this in Ecclesiastes 2:1–11:

> I said to myself, "Come now, I will test you with pleasure to find out what is good." But that also proved to be meaningless. "Laughter," I said, "is madness. And what does pleasure accomplish?" I tried cheering myself with wine, and embracing folly—my mind still guiding me with wisdom. I wanted to see what was good for people to do under the heavens during the few days of their lives.
>
> I undertook great projects: I built houses for myself

and planted vineyards. I made gardens and parks and planted all kinds of fruit trees in them. I made reservoirs to water groves of flourishing trees. I bought male and female slaves and had other slaves who were born in my house. I also owned more herds and flocks than anyone in Jerusalem before me. I amassed silver and gold for myself, and the treasure of kings and provinces. I acquired male and female singers, and a harem as well—the delights of a man's heart. I became greater by far than anyone in Jerusalem before me. In all this my wisdom stayed with me.

I denied myself nothing my eyes desired;
>I refused my heart no pleasure.

My heart took delight in all my labor,
>and this was the reward for all my toil.

Yet when I surveyed all that my hands had done
>and what I had toiled to achieve,

everything was meaningless, a chasing after the wind;
>nothing was gained under the sun.

He then concludes his thoughts at the end of the book with this:

Now all has been heard;
>here is the conclusion of the matter:

Fear God and keep his commandments,
>for this is the duty of all mankind.

For God will bring every deed into judgment,
    including every hidden thing,
    whether it is good or evil."

(Ecclesiastes 12:13–14)

We will discuss in detail why homosexuality is prohibited in scripture in a later study, but as a person who had a boyfriend for ten years and lived his life in and out of gay hangouts for years, but who has also spent decades dedicated to following Christ, I think I can speak with some authority on this issue: I can honestly say that fearing God and keeping his commandments is the greatest thing I have ever done with my life. It has not been easy, but it's been worth it. And I have reasoned that the benefits of following God far outweigh anything that homosexuality (or anything else) could ever do for me, and so it only makes logical sense to follow God's ways. Just being able to have the forgiveness of sins . . . how can one put a price on such a treasure?

Titus 2:11–14 puts it like this:

For the grace of God has appeared that offers salvation to all people. It teaches us to say "No" to ungodliness and worldly passions, and to live self-controlled, upright and godly lives in this present age, while we wait for the blessed hope—the appearing of the glory of our great God and Savior, Jesus Christ, who gave himself for us to redeem us from all wickedness and to purify for himself a people that are his very own, eager to do what is good.

As you go through these Bible studies, I hope you will discover, as I did, that the grace of God, as revealed and experienced through Jesus, is so amazing, so fulfilling, so wonderful, that it is worth giving up whatever you need to in order to become a Christian. The decisions you will be confronted with will not be easy, but *you can do this.* How do I know you can do it? I know it because God promises to equip us to follow him. I know it from my own experience. And I know it because numerous other same-sex attracted men and women have also chosen to live in obedience to the scriptures. But the choice is yours. God, the gentleman, wouldn't have it any other way.

"Now what I am commanding you today is not too difficult for you or beyond your reach. It is not up in heaven, so that you have to ask, "Who will ascend into heaven to get it and proclaim it to us so we may obey it?" Nor is it beyond the sea, so that you have to ask, "Who will cross the sea to get it and proclaim it to us so we may obey it?" No, the word is very near you; it is in your mouth and in your heart so you may obey it.

See, I set before you today life and prosperity, death and destruction. For I command you today to love the LORD your God, to walk in obedience to him, and to keep his commands, decrees and laws; then you will live and increase, and the LORD your God will bless you in the land you are entering to possess.

But if your heart turns away and you are not obedient, and if you are drawn away to bow down to other gods and worship them, I declare to you this day that you will certainly be destroyed. You will not live long in the land you are crossing the Jordan to enter and possess.

This day I call the heavens and the earth as witnesses against you that I have set before you life and death, blessings and curses. Now choose life, so that you and your children may live and that you may love the LORD your God, listen to his voice, and hold fast to him."

(Deuteronomy 30:11–20)

Discussion Questions for Study One

1. It's a popular notion today that if something feels right or natural, one should go ahead and do as they desire, as long as it doesn't hurt anyone else. This is especially true when it comes to the issue of homosexuality. Many will argue that because homosexuals were "born this way" (science has yet to prove definitively that there is a genetic cause for homosexuality) they should not be inhibited from celebrating that life and living it to the full. Speaking as a same-gender attracted man, I will tell you that I'm actually wide open to the possibility that genetics does indeed play a role in the

causation of homosexuality. If that fact is ever to be actually definitively proven, I fail to see how that would change my desire to follow the Biblical sexual ethic. My ability to choose how I will live and think, regardless of whether it feels right or natural or is even genetic has not changed. Just because something comes naturally to me does not mean I can't choose another path. We are not slaves to our DNA. How do you feel about this reality?

2. Can you appreciate the gift God has given us to have the freedom of choice? Do you see that you cannot have the freedom of choice without the freedom to refuse? For those who say they "must" follow the path of homosexuality because it feels natural, or is even genetically caused, do you see how they are giving up their God given right to choose how they will live? When this happens, people become enslaved to homosexuality. Where's the freedom in that?

Someone once argued with me that the animal kingdom proves that homosexuality is natural and even genetically caused because animals will often have sex with the same gender of their species. My response is that animals have no ability to choose; they're animals. It's not a moral issue to them. Following instinct is all they know. Humans are different, and this is what separates us from the animal kingdom. Humans can choose their path based on morality. For humans to be expected to participate in any activity based on instinct, feelings and emotions lowers us to that of the animal kingdom, which I would think we would all agree is quite an insult. What are your thoughts on this?

Study One Notes:

_____
_____
_____
_____
_____
_____
_____
_____
_____
_____
_____
_____
_____
_____
_____
_____
_____
_____
_____
_____
_____
_____
_____
_____
_____

STUDY TWO

Holiness, Not Heterosexuality, Part 1

Scriptures used in this study:

1 Corinthians 6:9–11

Hebrews 4:15

John 16:33

Proverbs 24:16

1 Thessalonians 5:23–24

Well, we might as well start by jumping "right into the deep end," as the saying goes. The question is: can a Christian be gay, lesbian or a homosexual? Well, it depends on what your definition of those words are. When we ask such a question, what we're talking about is sexual identity, and sexual identity is when we actively label ourselves based on our sexual preferences. This kind of self-identification is a relatively new phenomenon to the human experience that began in the mid-twentieth century. Since its inception, and especially in the last thirty years, our culture has elevated sexual identity to a place of high importance. Our culture values the idea of people labeling, self-identifying, and advertising themselves based upon their sexual preferences.

The words "gay," "homosexual," "lesbian," "same-sex attracted," and other related terms mean different things to different people. So let's begin by defining the words we are using in this study series so that we are all on the same page.

Dr. Mark A. Yarhouse (a psychologist with a PsyD and MA in Clinical Psychology, an MA in Theological Studies, and a PhD in Clinical Psychology) distinguishes between the terms "same-sex attraction" and "homosexual" in a way that I feel is extremely beneficial in this discussion in his book *Sexual Identity: A Guide to Living in the Time Between the Times:*

> At the first level, the most descriptive level, some people experience same-sex attraction. It does not necessarily mean anything more than that: it is an experience that they have, and some people experience opposite-sex attractions, while others report experiencing both same- and opposite-sex attractions.... Our experience is that this is the most accurate and helpful level of explanation and meaning-making for most people who experience homosexual attraction.... If Joe experiences same-sex attraction, it is more accurate and more helpful for him to say of himself, "I am a man who also experiences same-sex attractions," rather than to say of himself, "I am gay." The latter suggests he is a male and that his identity rests not in his gender but in his experiences of same-sex attraction. It also suggests something about same-sex behavior being a normal expression of who he

is as a person. The first way of describing himself, that is, to say, "I am a man who also experiences same-sex attraction," is merely descriptive, and it says nothing implicit about what the experiences of same-sex attraction means and what moral conclusions can be drawn from acting upon the attractions.[2]

Compare then the definition of "same-sex attraction" to those who have a "gay identity" or an identity of being a "homosexual":

[They] are those who integrate their experiences of same-sex attraction into a "gay" identity. That is, they speak of themselves with respect to a self-defining attribution, "I am gay," and this identity implicitly communicates something about how they view same-sex behavior, most often as a natural expression of who they are as a person...

...In contrast to the person who experiences same-sex attraction...for whom same-sex behavior is still under moral scrutiny; the other could integrate his experiences into a "gay identity," which carries with it the connotation that he celebrates same-sex behavior as a moral good, a natural extension of what it means to experience his sexual self-actualization in relation to himself and to others.[3]

It is for this reason that I do not consider myself to be a homosexual or gay. While I used to live like this, I do not (by my own free will and choice) any longer live like a person who actively engages in homosexual relationships. I do not "celebrate same-sex behavior as a moral good or a natural extension of what it means to experience [my] sexual self-actualization in relation to [myself] and others." This is not my identity, and therefore I am not a homosexual. Also, I do not describe myself with those terms because using the terms "gay" or "homosexual" will communicate something to most people that I have no intention of communicating—namely, that I am still involved in active homosexual behavior, which I am not.

I do, however, live with same-gender attractions, even though I have committed myself to not entertaining those appetites. I have *chosen* to walk along another path as I strive to follow Jesus. This would also be the case for the vast majority of Christians who come from a homosexual past or who have lived the majority of their lives sexually and emotionally attracted to the same gender. Since becoming a Christian, their attractions have not changed (for the most part), but *the way they choose to live their lives* has changed.

The Bible makes a clear distinction between people who are active homosexuals (that is, individuals who revel in the homosexual lifestyle and who hold no moral objections to it), versus people who, because of their understanding of Scripture, are not actively engaged in homosexuality.

In 1 Corinthians 6:9–11 the Bible says:

"Or do you not know that wrongdoers will not inherit the kingdom of God? Do not be deceived: Neither the sexually immoral nor idolaters nor adulterers nor men who have sex with men nor thieves nor the greedy nor drunkards nor slanderers nor swindlers will inherit the kingdom of God. And that is what some of you were. But you were washed, you were sanctified, you were justified in the name of the Lord Jesus Christ and by the Spirit of our God."

According to these words authored by Paul, it is the "wrongdoers" who will not inherit the kingdom of God. The apostle then goes on to explain who the wrongdoers are and then points out several categories; homosexuality being one of many. The scripture also goes on to explain that this is what some of them "were"—past tense.

They repented of their active participation in these sins—whether those sins were stealing, or greed or homosexuality—and they were now justified in the name of Jesus: they were washed, they were new people. It's not that they would never experience temptations or desires to act out in these areas again; it's that they would make it their goal in life to not to do them.

Is a Christian to be labeled a thief if he is tempted to steal but refuses to shoplift because of his commitment to God? No. Is a Christian to be labeled a liar if she is tempted to lie but strives daily to tell the truth because of her love for Jesus? No. Is a Christian, then, to be labeled a homosexual if he or she is tempted to be sexually involved with a member of the same gender, or is attracted to the same sex physically and emotionally, but refuses to give into those temptations and commit homosexual acts because of their commitment to godly purity and righteousness? No. The answer is "no" in every single scenario because the reality is that for the disciple of Jesus, our identity is Christ, not our sexual orientation or any other defining mark. Therefore, for the disciple of Jesus who is homo-erotically attracted, they are not gay or homosexual or lesbian; they are simply Christians.

The orientation of being "same-gender attracted" is, in and of itself, neither good nor bad; it just is. It is not a sin that I am same-sex attracted any more than it is a sin that someone else is opposite-sex attracted. Left alone, these terms are neutral.

Hebrews 4:15 says that "we do not have a high priest who is unable to sympathize with our weaknesses, but we have one who has been tempted in every way, just as we are—yet he did not sin" (NIV).

Christ experienced sexual temptation, meaning that there were times when he really wanted to sin sexually, and based on Hebrews 4:15, would it not be possible for us to consider that Christ also could have experienced homoerotic temptations as well? I recognize that Hebrews 4:15 is more of a general statement than a literal truth. It's most probable that Christ did not literally experience every temptation known to mankind, but one thing we can say with certainty is, that regardless of whatever temptations he did undergo, he did not sin, and that would include homosexual temptation, if indeed, he experienced such a thing.

Experiencing a homoerotic attraction is not sinful, just as experiencing heterosexual attractions is not sinful. Both attractions occur automatically and are involuntary. The key issue is what we do with the attraction; it is our actions that are either sinful or holy.

What kind of expectations should you have in regard to your sexual orientation if you decide to become a Christian? Well, I have never met anyone who willingly chose to be attracted to the same gender, and I have never met anyone who has completely changed their sexual orientation from being homosexually attracted to heterosexually attracted. I'm open to the fact that change in degrees is possible, but if your expectation is that this same-gender attraction will completely leave you, then I think that is unrealistic.

I do think it's possible that if you decide to become a Christian, over time you might experience diminished attractions to the same gender, to some degree. But I would suggest that a more important change would be that you will learn to place less emphasis on your sexuality overall. Your sexuality will always play an important part of your life, but it will never again be an identity marker for you.

Regardless, there is no such thing as a struggle-free life. To think that you can live a life that is conflict-free is impractical.

What is practical is finding new ways of dealing with the struggles you face.

Jesus said in John 16:33:

> "I have told you these things, so that in me you may have peace. In this world you will have trouble. But take heart! I have overcome the world" (NIV).

The attractions you experience to the same gender may or may not ever diminish, and you will not do any of this perfectly, but don't use these things as your measure of success. Aim to succeed in loving God and experiencing the peace that only he can provide, even in the midst of your struggle.

Being a same-sex attracted Christian has not been easy. I have experienced setbacks and failures, especially in my first few years as a Christian. But Proverbs 24:16 (NLT) says, "The godly may trip seven times, but they will get up again." Your responsibility after falling is to get up again, receive God's forgiveness, and keep moving forward.

What we choose to do with failure is perhaps the most profound indicator of who we are and who we will become. Failure can be a frustrating setback. You may try and fail sometimes and have a few setbacks but if you stay honest and determined, get help from Christian friends and God, you can do this! The greatest failure you could ever experience is quitting.

1 Thessalonians 5:23–24 says:

"Now may the God of peace make you holy in every way, and may your whole spirit and soul and body be kept blameless until our Lord Jesus Christ comes again. God will make this happen, for he who calls you is faithful" (NLT).

You see, this is the most exciting part of having holiness as your ultimate goal. When you become a Christian, God does all the work in the spiritual realm. He promises to make you holy, and keep you holy and blameless until Jesus comes back again. We do our part by doing our best and not quitting; God does his part by forgiving us when we fall and keeping us holy and blameless until the end. In other words, as long as you don't quit but keep relying on God, you can't lose.

Discussion Questions for Study Two

1. How do you feel about letting go of the identity markers you have been using ("gay," "homosexual," "transgender," "lesbian," etc.) and allowing Christ to be your identity?

2. Gay affirming churches have no problem with a "Christian" being actively involved in homosexuality. Indeed, this is their primary purpose of existence, allowing people to have their cake and eat it too! How do you feel about living your life as a true Christian who is same-gender attracted, but glorifying God with your life by not being actively involved in homosexuality in order to follow the Biblical sexual ethic?

3. Considering Proverbs 24:16, discuss this quote from this study; "What we choose to do with failure is perhaps the most profound indicator of who we are and who we will become."

Study Two Notes:

_____
_____
_____
_____
_____
_____
_____
_____
_____
_____
_____
_____
_____
_____
_____
_____
_____
_____
_____
_____
_____

STUDY THREE
Holiness, Not Heterosexuality, Part 2

Scriptures used in this study:

2 Timothy 2:20

1 Peter 2:9–12

Galatians 3:26–27

1 Timothy 2:21

1 Corinthians 10:31

Psalm 37: 3-7

1 Corinthians 6:17

1 John 2:15–17

A s someone who grew up going to church, I am very familiar with the term *holiness*. However, to be honest, the meaning seems so grandiose and utopian that it's true definition has often eluded me. I think that one of the biggest problems we face in achieving holiness is that we really don't understand what it is.

When I was young, my church (and my parents) taught that holiness meant not dancing, or gambling, or playing any kind of card game (even if it was a children's game), or playing pool, or drinking any kind of alcohol in any kind of setting for any reason whatsoever, and a whole long list of other no-nos. (Yeah, it wasn't a lot of fun!)

On the other hand, holiness included a lot of to-dos like reading your Bible, praying, paying your tithes, going to church every time the doors were open, and on and on. To sum it all up, holiness was a long list of "dos and don'ts." And if you did the dos, and didn't do the don'ts, then you were "holy."

In the Bible, *holiness* actually means "separated," "set apart," or "different."

In Canadian homes our mothers have the "everyday dishes" and then the "good dishes." I'm sure most cultures can relate to this idea in some way. The good dishes are usually kept in a cabinet on display somewhere because they're so beautiful. As a kid, when I wanted to make a snack or grab a bite to eat, I didn't dare use the good dishes—not if I wanted to live to see the next day, anyway. I had to use one of the everyday dishes. You see, the good dishes only came out on special occasions, usually when there was company around to impress. These dishes were "set apart" for a special purpose. They were separated. They were not stored with, or treated like, the ordinary dishes. These were special dishes.

Paul talks about these kinds of dishes in 2 Timothy 2:20:

"In a wealthy home some utensils are made of gold and silver, and some are made of wood and clay. The expensive utensils are used for special occasions, and the cheap ones are for everyday use" (NLT).

In the New King James Version it says it like this: "some for honor and some for dishonor."

So living a life of holiness means living a life that is separated, or set apart. It means that Christians are not like ordinary people. They are a special people. Not *better*, just *special*.

This means that true disciples of Jesus *are not free* to live any way they desire. Peter points this out:

> But you are a chosen people, a royal priesthood, a holy nation, God's special possession, that you may proclaim the praises of him who called you out of darkness into his wonderful light. Once you were not a people, but now you are the people of God; once you had not received mercy, but now you have received mercy.
>
> Dear friends, I urge you, as foreigners and exiles, to abstain from evil desires, which wage war against your soul. Live such good lives among the pagans that, though they accuse you of doing wrong, they may see your good deeds and glorify God on the day he visits us (1 Peter 2:9–12 NIV).

And just in case people forget, Peter lists the things that God has done for Christians. He talks of the darkness they were once in, and how they now live in light. And in case any of the people want to be arrogant about their holy or separated status,

Peter is quick to point out that they have received God's mercy. That is, they deserve destruction just like everyone else. They cannot be arrogant, because they have not made themselves to be what they are. They are where they are only because of the mercy of God.

True holiness should pervade every aspect of the Christian's life, impacting their every decision and action. But holiness also involves righteousness. Here's how: Before a person was saved, they engaged in all kinds of filthy behavior, they did all kinds of dishonorable and dirty things but it didn't make a difference, because at that time they were separated from God. In fact, they were God's enemies. But after a person is saved, they put on these spiritually clean clothes and because of their unique position in the spiritual realm, they are now expected to do the best they can to keep those clothes clean.

The person dressed in clean and expensive clothes wouldn't dream of climbing into a pen with pigs. The person wearing an expensive suit or a dress and high heels wouldn't dream of going out into a field to farm. The clothes are just too expensive. In the same way, followers of Jesus are wearing the spiritual clothes of a Christian, and they need to do all they can to keep those clothes clean.

Galatians 3:26–27 (NIV) puts it like this: "So in Christ Jesus you are all children of God through faith, for all of you who were baptized into Christ have clothed yourselves with Christ." And 2 Timothy 2:21 (NLT) says, "If you keep yourself pure, you will be a special utensil for honorable use. Your life will be clean, and you will be ready for the Master to use you for every good work."

You see, in order for us to remain separated for God's special use, we must remain pure. A Christian is a separated person. He or she is separated unto God, not because of anything they have done—God forbid that *they* consider themselves special because of anything they have done or accomplished. The disciple of Jesus is only separated because they have been made pure by the blood of Jesus.

Before becoming a Christian, my focus was on watching out for Number One: me, myself, and I. So I lied, stole, looked down on others, was greedy, and participated in all kinds of sexual activity to protect myself and make sure my needs were met. After I became a Christian, Jesus became Number One. When that happened, all of my priorities changed. I could no longer live life for my glory, but for Jesus' glory. As it says in 1 Corinthians 10:31 (NIV), "So whether you eat or drink or whatever you do, do it all for the glory of God."

I believe we must make the connection that controlling our passions and acting like the man or woman God created us to be (in other words, *being holy*) honors the Lord. No other reason could compel us to change our lives the way we do. We should want to be righteous in every area of our lives for one reason: because we desire to be holy. We should want to conquer our homosexual temptations for one reason: because we desire to be holy. Not because we're tired of the fight, not because it will help save our marriage, not because we are afraid of people finding out, not because we want to be "normal" (whatever that is!), not because we want to please anyone else… but *only* because we want to honor God by being holy. That is why the goal of your life, if you become a Christian, is not to eradicate your homosexual temptations, or your same-gender attractions. Your goal in life is holiness.

If your attraction to the same sex leaves you someday, then count yourself blessed and praise God. But please know that your worth to God and his love for you have absolutely nothing to do with your sexual orientation. Whether you are attracted to a man or to a woman, I do not believe God looses any sleep over… What he does care about is that you choose to be holy for him, regardless of what kind of temptations you face. God is glorified in the daily choices we make to turn away from gratifying our flesh and our sinful fantasies, in whatever manner they present themselves.

> Trust in the Lord, and do good. . . .
> Take delight in the LORD,
>   and he will give you the desires of your heart.
>
> Commit your way to the LORD;
>   trust also in him, and he will do this:
> He will make your righteousness shine like the dawn,
>   your vindication like the noonday sun.
>
> Be still before the LORD and wait patiently for him.
> (Psalm 37:3–7 NIV)

Do you long to be the man or woman God would have you to be? Then our motivation must be that we are holy, separate for God, useful to him, not just that we are sinless or religious or following a list of "do's" and "don'ts."

The bottom line is that sin is pleasurable for a season, but it leaves stains that make it better left alone. We need to learn the lesson that if we follow Jesus, and truly strive for holiness, we won't miss the sinful pleasures, because we know that our holiness—our "separateness"—gives us access to pleasures that far surpass any temporary satisfactions that our old sinful life could ever provide.

Consider what Paul says in 2 Corinthians 6:17 (NLT):

> "'Therefore, come out from among unbelievers, and separate yourselves from them, says the LORD. Don't touch their filthy things, and I will welcome you.' "

The way to holiness is not to try to hold on to a little bit of the world while trying to be righteous or religious. The way to holiness is not to live a half-hearted, half-in, half-out kind of Christianity. The way to holiness is not to have cafeteria-style Christianity where you pick and choose what you will believe and follow, and what you won't. The way to holiness is to "come out from them and separate yourselves from them."

I am fully aware of the kind of commitment and complete lifestyle change we are talking about here. I am aware, because I have done it myself! If you have been actively living a gay life, then we are most likely talking about you changing the dynamic of a relationship with a gay partner. We are talking about you no longer acting out in any kind of homosexual activity. We are talking about you no longer celebrating a way of life that you have celebrated for many years. I know it's a lot. But let me ask you, aren't you tired of being lied to?

Satan pretends to be something that he is not. He tries to sell us goods and products that promise abundance but that eventually deliver additional spiritual and emotional baggage never advertised. He takes something that is evil and that will ultimately poison us spiritually and he makes it appear satisfying and enjoyable—for the moment. This is how Satan plays mind games with humanity. In a thousand different ways, Satan tries to sell us pleasures—heterosexual relationships, homosexual relationships, drugs, wealth, any number of things—that fall far short of what God wants for us. And worst of all, Satan's "gifts" have horrible dangers hidden in the fine print . . . dangers that only hurt us in the end.

> Do not love this world nor the things it offers you, for when you love the world, you do not have the love of the Father in you. For the world offers only a craving for physical pleasure, a craving for everything we see, and pride in our achievements and possessions. These are not from the Father, but are from this world. And this world is fading away, along with everything that

people crave. But anyone who does what pleases God will live forever.

(1 John 2:15–17 NLT)

Discussion Questions for Study Three

1. How does being "set apart" for Christ inspire you to live differently?

2. What lifestyle changes would be necessary for you to truly strive for a holy life and follow Christ?

3. Discuss this quote from this study; "We should want to conquer our homosexual temptations for one reason: because we desire to be holy. Not because we're tired of the fight, not because it will help save our marriage, not because we are afraid of people finding out, not because we want to be "normal" (whatever that is!), not because we want to please anyone else…but only because we want to honor God by being holy. That is why the goal of your life, if you become a Christian, is not to eradicate your homosexual temptations or your same-gender attractions. Your goal in life is holiness."

Study Three Notes:

_____

_____

_____

_____

_____

_____

_____

_____

_____

_____

_____

_____

_____

_____

_____

_____

_____

_____

_____

_____

_____

_____

_____

_____

STUDY FOUR
God, the Architect of the Heart

Scriptures used in this study:

Leviticus 18:22

Leviticus 20:13

Romans 1:26–27

1 Corinthians 6:9–10

1 Timothy 1:9–11

John 21:25

Ezra 10:11

Psalm 139:1–18

Ever hear of John Najjar? Probably not. Ever hear of the 1965 Ford Mustang? Yeah, a classic, right? It's not hard to argue that it's one of the most famous cars ever put into a show-

room. Well, John Najjar was the designer of that car; he is even the one who came up with the cool name.

In 1936, John Najjar was working on the assembly line at

Ford as a machinist. One day Henry Ford—yeah, THE Henry Ford—came walking by and asked Najjar if he liked his job. John Najjar responded, "I'd rather be drawing cars than making them." The next day, Najjar was transferred to the design department, working alongside Edsel Ford, Henry's son. Over the years, John Najjar was responsible for designing some of the greatest cars that Ford ever put on the road, including the Lincoln Continental. But nothing comes close to the car he loved designing the most: the first Mustang.

That car was amazing. It had a 280 CI engine under the hood with 210 horsepower, it could go from 0 to 60 mph in 7.5 seconds, and it could do a quarter mile in 15 seconds at 89 miles an hour. This classic car didn't hit the showroom until mid-1964, but John Najjar started designing it in 1961. It took years of painstaking work that Najjar considered a labor of love. But it was all worth it, and every car enthusiast in the world and every person who gets behind the wheel of a Ford Mustang will forever be indebted to a guy by the name of John Najjar.

Why are we speaking of this man? Because he would be horrified if you were to take his baby and use it in a way that destroyed it. Put sugar in the gas tank, drain the oil and let the engine run, drive it off a cliff, submerge it in water, or do any number of dumb things to the car that it wasn't designed for, and you would destroy Najjar's incredible creation. No longer would it be able to go 0 to 60 mph in 7.5 seconds. Why? Because regardless of the care and detail that went into designing the vehicle, it wasn't designed to run on sugar or be driven into a pool of water. To do so would be to use the vehicle for something it was never intended.

And this is what sin does to the human heart and body. Do you know what the word *sin* actually means? "To miss the mark." That's it. When we sin in any way, we are missing the mark of what God intended for us to do with our minds and bodies. God, as the creator of the universe and great architect of our hearts and souls, was painstakingly precise in putting us together. He designed us to be used in specific ways. Just as the 1965 Ford Mustang could be easily destroyed if not used in the manner that the designer intended, so it is with the human being. Take a person's body, mind and soul and use them and abuse them in ways that the designer never intended, and you will ruin them, sometimes irreversibly.

When Ford put out the first Mustang, it came with an owner's manual to tell the owner how to get the best performance out of the vehicle. God has an owner's manual too. It's called the Bible, and in it, he clearly explains how to best treat ourselves and others so that we can get the most out of life. This spiritual owner's manual may include a list of "dos and don'ts," but not because God is authoritative or mean, or enjoys "lording it" over people (no pun intended). The rules in the manual exist because he is our designer and architect, and he knows what will work and what will destroy. And one of the activities that will destroy our lives is any kind of sexual activity outside of the boundaries of a man and woman united together in marriage. Stepping outside those bounds will ultimately cause damage to our lives and souls, so the owner's manual tells us not to do it. Stepping outside those boundaries would obviously include homosexuality.

The Bible confronts homosexuality directly five times, and in each occasion, it calls it sinful.

> Do not lie with a man as one lies with a woman; that is detestable.
>
> (Leviticus 18:22)

> If a man lies with a man as one lies with a woman, both of them have done what is detestable...
>
> (Leviticus 20:13)

> Because of this, God gave them over to shameful lusts. Even their women exchanged natural relations for unnatural ones. In the same way the men also abandoned natural relations with women and were inflamed with lust for one another. Men committed indecent acts with other men, and received in themselves the due penalty for their perversion.
>
> (Romans 1:26-27)

> Do you not know that the wicked will not inherit the kingdom of God? Do not be deceived: Neither the sexually immoral nor idolaters nor adulterers nor male prostitutes nor homosexual offenders nor thieves nor

the greedy nor drunkards nor slanderers nor swindlers will inherit the kingdom of God.

(1 Corinthians 6:9-10)

We also know that law is made not for the righteous but for lawbreakers and rebels, the ungodly and sinful, the unholy and irreligious; for those who kill their fathers or mothers, for murderers, for adulterers and perverts, for slave traders and liars and perjurers—and for whatever else is contrary to the sound doctrine that conforms to the glorious gospel of the blessed God, which he entrusted to me.

(1 Timothy 1:9-11)

Even though the Old Testament mentions and even allows other kinds of relationships (like polygamy and the use of concubines), the Bible upholds a monogamous relationship between husband and wife as the standard. Whereas heterosexuality is commended throughout the Bible, not once is a homosexual relationship mentioned in anything but negative terms.

Let's address some common objections and questions that people have about homosexuality:

1. **Some will ask, "Okay, Guy, but what if I was born this way? How can homosexuality be a sin if this is how God created me?"**

The purpose of this study is not to focus on causation, but I will say here that I think that people who debate over whether or not there is a genetic cause for homosexuality spend too much time doing so. The truth is, no one yet knows for sure what causes homosexuality. When this booklet was being written, science has yet to prove definitively that there is a genetic cause, and the Bible does not speak to it. I'm open to the fact that someday a "genetic-explanation gene" will be found, but as of right now, it hasn't.

That being said, as a same-sex attracted man, I will tell you that it certainly *feels* like I was born this way. I know that I never made a conscious choice to be attracted to the same gender, and it's all I've ever known since I was about eleven years old. I don't know if I was born like this or not, but quite frankly, for the Christian, I don't think it matters. Because the Christian is devoted to following the spiritual "owner's manual," this matter gets resolved very quickly, because nowhere in Scripture does God say that homosexuality is permissible if it can be proven that it is caused by genetics alone. And the same principle holds true for *all* sin, not just homosexuality! In the same way, it never says in Scripture, "Thou shall not lie, unless, of course, there is a genetic cause for your deceit, in which case, lie your brains out." Maybe one day it will be discovered scientifically that lying is an inborn trait. All right, *even if that's true*, I'm still going to do all I can to teach my kids not to lie, because deceit only causes hurt, damage, and chaos in their lives.

2. **"But Guy," some argue, "Jesus said nothing about homosexuality."**

It's true that we do not have any record of Jesus speaking on this topic. But in order to use that as your argument in favor of homosexuality, you would also have to argue that the Gospels are more authoritative than the rest of the Bible (where homosexuality is explicitly forbidden). But the Gospel writers never claimed that their books should be elevated above the Torah or any of the other writings that comprise the New Covenant. Besides, the idea of a subject being unimportant just because it was not mentioned by Jesus does not make sense. Are we to believe that Jesus did not care about wife-beating or incest, just because he said nothing about them? There are any number of sinful behaviors that Christ did not mention by name; surely we don't condone them for that reason alone! Also, John 21:25 says, "Jesus did many other things as well. If every one of them were written down, I suppose that even the whole world would not have room for the books that would be written." Just because we do not have a record of Jesus forbidding homosexual behavior, does not mean he never did.

3. **Others argue, "The scriptures that condemn homosexuality have actually been mistranslated."**

It's true that we can find some discrepancy in minor areas of translation in the Bible, but on a topic as important as sexual ethics, are we really to believe that the Bible translators we rely on got it wrong *five* different times, in *two* different Testaments, and *only* in the passages regarding homosexuality? (Pro-gay apologists have no problem with the other scriptures condemning sins like adultery and child abuse.)

4. **Some say, "Bible verses which seem to prohibit homosexuality have actually been yanked out of context from their original meaning, or else they only applied to the culture existing at the time they were written."**

The scriptures about homosexuality are clear and simple. For example, "Do not lie with a man as one lies with a woman; that is detestable" (Leviticus 18:22) requires no more interpretation than the clear-cut command, "You shall not murder" (Exodus 20:13). As for the "out of context" argument, it simply isn't true. In Leviticus, Romans, 1 Corinthians and 1 Timothy, homosexuality is mentioned in the context of sexual and immoral behavior! The context is quite clear. A variety of behaviors are prohibited, including homosexuality, along with heterosexual sins such as adultery, fornication, and idolatry. Homosexuality is only one of many sins.

5. **"My partner and I are in a monogamous relationship, and we truly love each other."**

This is another fine-sounding argument intended to show why homosexuality should be allowable by God. The problem with that line of reasoning is that love in and of itself does not make a relationship right. An unmarried heterosexual Christian couple may be very much in love, but if they become sexually involved before marriage, it will still be sin, regardless of how sincere the love is. A married man can fall deeply in love with a woman other than his wife. The love may be genuine, but that does not make it right in God's eyes, and the consequences of a relationship like this would be life-altering for everyone involved.

Joe Dallas has authored a very helpful book called *The Gay Gospel* (Harvest House, 2007), a resource I've used for this study. I highly recommend it if you're interested in learning more about what he calls "Pro-Gay Theology." In his book, these arguments and many others are discussed and refuted.

Let me discuss the issue of gay marriage. Clearly this is one of the most controversial and difficult issues that we must address—it is difficult because it is so emotional. The reality is, two men or two women who are entwined in a monogamous, intimate, and caring relationship can be genuinely and deeply in love with one another. How should a gay, married couple who are interested in becoming Christians deal with their situation? Things grow even more complicated when children are involved. How should this couple proceed? The answers are not easy, and I'm sure there are many who would disagree with me, but here is where I have landed on it.

The question has to be asked: is it possible for a gay, married couple who are enmeshed in a romantic relationship to continue to live in the same dwelling as followers of Jesus? I can't imagine how. Some argue (especially if there are children involved) that this couple could continue to live under the same roof, provided that they commit to no longer being sexually involved with one another; they suggest that for the sake of the children, this would be a viable option.

While I understand the reasons for this suggestion, I personally disagree with the logic. Just because two people agree to no longer have a sexual relationship does not mean that everything is right in God's eyes. If a heterosexual, married man were involved in a romantic relationship with a woman at work, but then decided to end the sex but retain the friendship and the constant contact at work…well, that idea wouldn't fly at home with his wife. The man's wife would not be thrilled about the relationship continuing, even if there were no longer a sexual component to it. The same principle holds true in the gay marriage situation. If two men or two women were committed to no longer being involved sexually, but were still in love with one another, the relationship would still not be right.

I realize this is complex and painful, but for the gay married couple who want to be followers of Jesus, I see no other way for things to work. They will have to decide upon a complete separation, both emotionally and physically, even if children are involved.

This, of course, would take time and much planning and consideration, and I would encourage all involved to be patient as the details are sorted out.

The reality is, every living person has scrambled their own egg, we've all made mistakes that needed correcting before becoming a Christian; welcome to humanity! In this instance, God is not the one who scrambled this egg; the people involved are the ones who did that. With love, help, and support from other Christians, they would have to be the ones to try to unscramble things as best they could. My intention is not to sound insensitive or unkind, nor to take a simplistic approach to a complex and delicate situation—but all of us who want to follow Jesus have to make dramatic changes, and sometimes those changes are painful and difficult. When I became a Christian, I made the decision to break off a relationship of ten years with my boyfriend. It was not easy, but unfortunately, he was not interested in living for Jesus and following the biblical sexual ethic. I am the one who scrambled that egg, and so it was I who had to do all I could to make things right. If my boyfriend had decided to become a Christian, then he and I still would have had to break up. We would have had to commit to never again being involved with one another emotionally, romantically, or sexually.

I would also ask you to consider Ezra 10:11. You will see here how the holy priests of God had married foreign women— women who worshiped other gods and idols. As detestable as divorce was (and is) to God, he still demanded that the priests divorce these women in order to make things right, so that the priests could make themselves holy. Just as discussed in our last lesson, Christians are holy, set apart, just as these priests were.

In making such a difficult decision, I would also encourage you to look at this through the lens of glorifying God with your lives. You are separating, not because you "have to" or because the Bible says "you must," but because you want to glorify God with your lives, and making these choices (as hard as they are) will do just that. God is honored and glorified by your willingness to align your lives according to his will, for he is the master designer, the great architect. He will bless your steps of faith. He is the one who formed you and he is well aware of what will truly make you fulfilled, whole, and happy.

I conclude this chapter with these beautiful words about God's love for us:

O LORD, you have examined my heart
    and know everything about me.
You know when I sit down or stand up.
    You know my thoughts even when I'm far away.
You see me when I travel and when I rest at home.
    You know everything I do.
You know what I am going to say
    even before I say it, LORD.

You go before me and follow me.
    You place your hand of blessing on my head.
Such knowledge is too wonderful for me,
    too great for me to understand!

I can never escape from your Spirit!
    I can never get away from your presence!
If I go up to heaven, you are there;

if I go down to the grave, you are there.
If I ride the wings of the morning,
    if I dwell by the farthest oceans,
even there your hand will guide me,
    and your strength will support me.

I could ask the darkness to hide me
    and the light around me to become night—
but even in darkness I cannot hide from you.
    To you the night shines as bright as day.
Darkness and light are the same to you.

You made all the delicate, inner parts of my body
    and knit me together in my mother's womb.
Thank you for making me so wonderfully complex!
    Your workmanship is marvelous—how well I know it.
You watched me as I was being formed in utter seclusion,
    as I was woven together in the dark of the womb.
    You saw me before I was born.
Every day of my life was recorded in your book.
    Every moment was laid out before a single day had passed.

How precious are your thoughts about me, O God.
    They cannot be numbered!
I can't even count them;
    they outnumber the grains of sand!

(Psalm 139:1–18 NLT)

Discussion Questions for Study Four

1. How do you feel about the way God (your architect and designer) so carefully put you together?

2. What "eggs" have you scrambled in your life that need "unscrambling" and what practical steps need to be taken to do this?

Study Four Notes:

STUDY FIVE

Quenching Our Emotional Thirsts, Part 1

Scriptures used in this study:

John 4:7–29

Proverbs 27:20

Isaiah 55:1–3

A few years ago I was trying to find a way to best describe to a group of heterosexual Christians why (before I found Jesus) homosexuality had seemed so good to me. My example below is imperfect, I know, but I do think it gets the point across.

A study was done in 2013[4] to determine what drinking one can of Coke does to the body, within 60 minutes of consuming the drink. The study also points out that Coke is not the only culprit, but this process works the same way when people drink any "non-diet" soda. In short, this kind of drink "wreaks havoc on the human organism." The main problem is sugar . . .

In the first 10 minutes: Ten teaspoons of sugar hit your system (100 percent of your recommended daily intake). You don't immediately vomit from the overwhelming sweetness only because phosphoric acid cuts the flavor, allowing you to keep it down.

20 minutes: Your blood sugar spikes, causing an "insulin burst." Your liver responds to this by turning any sugar it can get its hands on into fat.

40 minutes: Caffeine absorption is complete. Your pupils dilate, your blood pressure rises. In response, your liver dumps *more sugar* into your bloodstream. The adenosine receptors in your brain are now blocked, preventing drowsiness.

45 minutes: Your body ups your dopamine production, stimulating the pleasure centers of your brain. (This is physically the same way heroin works, by the way.)

60 minutes: The phosphoric acid binds calcium, magnesium and zinc in your lower intestine, providing a further boost in metabolism. This is compounded by high doses of sugar and artificial sweeteners, also increasing the urinary excretion of calcium.

60 Minutes: The caffeine's diuretic properties come into play. (It makes you have to urinate.) It is now assured that you'll evacuate the bonded calcium, magnesium and zinc that were headed to your bones, as well as sodium, electrolytes and water.

60 minutes: As the rave inside of you dies down you'll start to have a sugar crash. You may become irritable and/or sluggish. You have also now urinated away all the water that was in the Coke—but not before infusing it with valuable nutrients your body could have used for things like even having the *ability* to hydrate your system, or build strong bones and teeth.

Considering this information, it's almost revolting to consider the persecution our bodily systems are suffering, all while we sit comfortably in our full-cushioned, high-back reclining chairs, each one providing its own personal cup holder large enough to hold cups the size of buckets. I think next time I go to a movie, I'll just ask for water!

The point is this: While the disturbing details listed here will most likely cause you to think twice the next time you reach for a soft drink, the truth is that we have always known that drinking a bottle of soda is bad for us. You didn't need a study to tell you that. You've always known that this stuff is just a mixture of sugar, coloring, and chemicals—chemicals like phosphoric acid (which, by the way, is also tremendous for the removal of rust from the bumper of your car).

The really fascinating thing is that even though we have known that these drinks are incredibly unhealthy, most of us still drink them. In fact, it's probably a safe bet to say that even though you have now been equipped with this information, sometime in the near future you will still drink another Coke and put your body into shock again. Why? Because on a hot sunny day or while you are watching something blow up on a gigantic movie screen, there are few things that taste better than an ice cold Coke! After all, "it's the real thing." Right?

You see, even though colas aren't good for us, they still quench our thirst, they still meet the need—even if it is only momentarily.

So what's so great about homosexuality? Why is it so alluring and so incredibly difficult to turn away from? Because for those who are same-gender attracted, it quenches thirst— emotional thirst, relational thirst, sexual thirst—even if only momentarily.

The first thing I want to point out as we begin this journey is that while we will be focusing specifically on issues pertaining to homosexuality, homosexuality by itself is not the real problem; it is merely one symptom of many that speak to the fact that we are all born into a broken world. *This is not a homosexual issue, this is a human issue.*

Every single living human being has turned to their own "drink" to get their needs met. And the needs are legitimate: loneliness, fear, anger, depression, sadness, emotional hunger, anxiety, hurt...the list goes on and on. The trouble is that Satan has tried to sell all of us products (take your pick) that promise to relieve these pains; but it's all a lie, a sham—a wealth of products that promise so much and deliver so little. What Satan offers is the greatest rip-off in the history of the world, and every one of us has spent time and money and been taken in, only to be left sorely disappointed. Homosexuality is just one of hundreds, if not thousands, of things that we as humans have turned to in order to get our "fix."

In John 4, we're given a prime example of this.

When a Samaritan woman came to draw water, Jesus said to her, "Will you give me a drink?" (His disciples had gone into the town to buy food.)

The Samaritan woman said to him, "You are a Jew and I am a Samaritan woman. How can you ask me for a drink?" (For Jews do not associate with Samaritans.)

Jesus answered her, "If you knew the gift of God and who it is that asks you for a drink, you would have asked him and he would have given you living water."

"Sir," the woman said, "you have nothing to draw with and the well is deep. Where can you get this living water? Are you greater than our father Jacob, who gave us the well and drank from it himself, as did also his sons and his flocks and herds?"

Jesus answered, "Everyone who drinks this water will be thirsty again, but whoever drinks the water I give them will never thirst. Indeed, the water I give them will become in them a spring of water welling up to eternal life."

The woman said to him, "Sir, give me this water so that I won't get thirsty and have to keep coming here to draw water."

He told her, "Go, call your husband and come back."

"I have no husband," she replied.

Jesus said to her, "You are right when you say you have no husband. The fact is, you have had five husbands, and the man you now have is not your husband. What you have just said is quite true."

"Sir," the woman said, "I can see that you are a prophet. Our ancestors worshiped on this mountain, but you Jews claim that the place where we must worship is in Jerusalem."

"Woman," Jesus replied, "believe me, a time is coming when you will worship the Father neither on this mountain nor in Jerusalem. You Samaritans worship what you do not know; we worship what we do know, for salvation is from the Jews. Yet a time is coming and has now come when the true worshipers will worship the Father in spirit and truth, for they are the kind of worshipers the Father seeks. God is spirit, and his worshipers must worship in spirit and in truth."

The woman said, "I know that Messiah" (called Christ) "is coming. When he comes, he will explain everything to us."

Then Jesus declared, "I, the one speaking to you—am he."

Just then his disciples returned and were surprised to find him talking with a woman. But no one asked, "What do you want?" or "Why are you talking with her?"

Then, leaving her water jar, the woman went back to the town and said to the people, "Come, see a man who told me everything I ever did." (John 4:7–29 NIV)

This is a story about a lonely and troubled woman who was trying desperately to quench a spiritual and emotional thirst. There was no permanent satisfaction in the multiple relationships she had experienced. In fact, each time a relationship ended, she needed to go and find a new mate, hoping that this next man would meet all of her emotional needs. Of course, this never worked, and is the very reason that the poor woman was now into her sixth relationship. Jesus told her that she would never truly be satisfied until she drank the kind of water that he had for her.

My life mirrors that woman's in many ways. There are few things that I have turned to in order to quench my emotional thirsts more than homosexuality. When I felt lonely, afraid or insecure, I turned to homosexuality to meet what were very legitimate needs. Mind you, I also went there because it was exciting and even satisfying, but there is one thing homosexuality never, ever was for me: fulfilling.

Like the woman that Jesus met, I was always left still thirsty. Illicit sex, pornography, gay bars, over-indulging in food and sleep and entertainment…the list goes on…those things may have been momentarily exciting and fun, but they never left me feeling satisfied in the long-term. In fact, I was only left feeling even thirstier, more empty and alone, forcing me to go and engage in all of those activities all over again—it was a vicious cycle.

Jesus offered this woman, and he offers you and me, something so much more satisfying than what we find in the other places we have so often gone. He offers us all "living water." And just as this woman would never find contentment in going from relationship to relationship, so it is with you and me. Homosexuality will never, ever give us what we really need or even want. It will always (one hundred percent of the time) leave us emotionally, relationally, and spiritually thirsty. Only when we decide to satisfy our thirst with the living water that Jesus offers us will we ever be truly satisfied.

Homosexuality deceived me, and I fell for it hook, line, and sinker! It promised me things that it was never able to deliver. Regardless of how hard I searched to quench my thirst—to find long-lasting peace and fulfillment—it never worked. Let me ask you: Did homosexuality quench your emotional thirsts? I mean, consider all that homosexuality promised us: happiness, satisfaction, fulfillment, love, acceptance, and even inner peace. Did it deliver these things for you? It did for me, but only for a short amount of time. It never gave me lasting fulfillment. I was always left needing more.

Before my conversion to Jesus, I "had to" keep crossing new lines, doing things I said I would never do, and involving myself more and more in homosexual activity. Every time I had sex with another man or participated in some kind of homosexual act, regardless of how much I enjoyed it at the time, I always ended up hating myself. Every time I would end up feeling angry and more alone. Even throughout the ten-year relationship I had with my boyfriend, deep down, I always felt like something was wrong. The thirst was never satisfied, regardless of what homosexuality had promised me.

Proverbs 27:20 says, "Death and destruction are never satisfied, and neither are human eyes." How has this been true in your life when it comes to homosexuality?

Are you tired of being lied to? Are you tired of being made a fool of by Satan? Are you exhausted from countless trips to a well of water that only leaves you thirstier to get your emotional needs met?

In Isaiah 55:1–3 we are asked a few good questions by God:

"Come, all you who are thirsty,
　　come to the waters;
and you who have no money,
　　come, buy and eat!
Come, buy wine and milk
　　without money and without cost.
Why spend money on what is not bread,
　　and your labor on what does not satisfy?
Listen, listen to me, and eat what is good,
　　and you will delight in the richest of fare.
Give ear and come to me;
　　listen, that you may live.
I will make an everlasting covenant with you,
　　my faithful love promised to David."

If you're anything like me, I spent a lot on homosexuality: a lot of time and energy wasted; hours, days, months, even years that I will never get back. Some of us have spent a lot of money, too, all to drink something that would never satisfy us to begin with. What a waste!

Do you not deserve better? God thinks so!

God calls out to you and me, and begs us to come to him so that our souls may live. What God offers is free. It will cost you nothing, and it is the only thing that will quench your hurts, fears, and insecurities.

Discussion Questions for Study Five

1. How does your life or experience mirror the story of the woman at the well? How has homosexuality lied to you?

2. How have you misspent yourself (emotionally, relationally, financially) on satisfying your needs through homosexuality?

3. What does Isaiah 55:1–3 mean to you?

4. What are you still doing, right now, that shows you are still going to the contaminated water of homosexuality to get your needs met?

5. Are you ready for change?

Study Five Notes

STUDY SIX

Quenching Our Emotional Thirsts, Part 2

Scriptures used in this study:

Jeremiah 2:13

Hebrews 4:12–13

2 Timothy 3:14–17

Proverbs 1:2–7

John 12:48

2 Corinthians 5:10

Ecclesiastes 12:11–14

Deuteronomy 20:11–30

I n our previous study we read the story of the woman at the well as recorded in John 4. Like all of us, she had numerous pains of the heart that needed healing, loneliness being only one of them. Like all of us, she was a broken person in a fallen world. Jesus described her as "thirsty." This woman, of course, was going to the wrong well to quench that thirst. She was going from relationship to relationship, only to be left thirstier than the time before. But then along came Jesus, pleading with her (and with us) to go to him for "living water" that would quench her (and our) emotional and spiritual thirst forever.

Is this not the story for each of us who come from a homosexual past or who have unwanted same-gender attractions? Every time we look with lust in our hearts; every time we allow an impure image, thought or memory to linger in our minds; every time we act out physically through masturbation or by actually having homosexual contact with someone else, we are going to the wrong drinking well, and we are only left thirstier than when we began.

Homosexuality deceived us. It has never provided what it promised, not in the long-term anyway. It may have provided some relief and gratification, but only for the short-term. But Jesus has now entered the picture, and he offers you something that is truly satisfying, something that will quench all of the pains of your heart: his living water. The story of this woman is so inspiring because as her interaction with Jesus comes to a close, we see that she leaves her water jug behind (John 4:28). While Scripture does not tell us exactly why she did this, I think it is symbolic of the fact that the vessel she had been using to draw water was no longer needed, because in Jesus she had found something better, and she knew it.

Are you willing to leave your water jug behind? Are you willing to leave homosexual relationships behind forever? Are you willing to do what it takes to get all the things Satan tries to sell us—fantasy, pornography, masturbation, gay bars, glory holes, gay hang-outs, drugs, alcohol, and the numerous other sinful, empty things—out of your life? Are you willing to take whatever steps are necessary to learn how to control your mind so that homosexual thoughts and memories are no longer allowed to live there? (I realize this list may not exactly mirror your struggles and sins, but if that's not your list, then what is?)

Remember this: You no longer need your old "water jugs" to give you water that will only leave you feeling thirstier. Jesus has something for you that will quench your thirst forever.

Jeremiah 2:13 tells us:

"My people have committed two sins: They have forsaken me, the spring of living water, and they have dug their own cisterns, broken cisterns that cannot hold water."

When we choose sin over God, we forsake God, the "spring of living water," and we then choose to dig our own cisterns—broken cisterns that cannot hold water. *This is not a homosexuality thing, this is a "sin" thing.* This is not a commentary on gays and lesbians, it's a commentary on broken humanity. Every single living human has dug their own cisterns—broken cisterns that cannot hold water.

When we turn to homosexuality in thought or in deed, we are drinking from a cistern that cannot hold water. Not only that, but when a cistern is broken, it doesn't just leak out the good water; it also allows the stinking, rancid outside water to come in. Please stop and consider what filthy water you have been allowing yourself to drink through homosexuality.

If you physically drank sewer water, imagine how terribly

ill you would become. None of us would dare do such a thing. Yet this is exactly what we are doing when we turn to activities that God, our creator, never meant for us to participate in. It makes us terribly ill and will eventually kill us off. Certainly this is true in the spiritual realm, and it is often true in the physical as well.

When I was involved in active homosexuality, I didn't view it this way at all. I didn't understand how I was damaging myself. In fact, there was a time when I liked homosexuality and what it did for me. But then, as he did for the woman at the well, Jesus entered my life and offered me something that was so much more quenching and satisfying. When I realized that he was offering me water that would gratify my emotional, relational and spiritual needs in a fulfilling and eternal way that homosexuality never could, Jesus became the obvious choice— the better well to draw my water from. I didn't leave homosexuality because I believed at the time that it was so terrible; I left homosexuality because I found something better. Homosexuality *did* provide what I was looking for, but only temporarily. Jesus quenched my thirst once and for all.

So it is the living water of God that we need. What is this "living water?"

> For the word of God is *living and active*. Sharper than any double-edged sword, it penetrates even to dividing soul and spirit, joints and marrow; it judges the thoughts and attitudes of the heart. Nothing in all creation is hidden

from God's sight. Everything is uncovered and laid bare before the eyes of him to whom we must give account.

(Hebrews 4:12–13, emphasis added)

But as for you, continue in what you have learned and have become convinced of, because you know those from whom you learned it, and how from infancy you have known the Holy Scriptures, which are able to make you wise for salvation through faith in Christ Jesus. All Scripture is God-breathed and is useful for teaching, rebuking, correcting and training in righteousness, so that the man of God may be thoroughly equipped for every good work.

(2 Timothy 3:14–17)

For attaining wisdom and discipline;
        for understanding words of insight;
for acquiring a disciplined and prudent life,
        doing what is right and just and fair;
for giving prudence to the simple,
        knowledge and discretion to the young—
let the wise listen and add to their learning,
        and let the discerning get guidance,
for understanding proverbs and parables,
        the sayings and riddles of the wise.

The fear of the LORD is the beginning of knowledge,

but fools despise wisdom and discipline.

(Proverbs 1:2–7)

And so, the choice is yours to make. Continue in homosexuality and the other sinful activities you have participated in, or repent and turn to God and make Jesus the Lord of your life. God, the perfect gentleman, will not force you. We as Christians and as your friends will not judge you (1 Corinthians 5:12). But all of us will have to pay the consequences of our choices and, in the end, answer to the Lord for our decisions.

"There is a judge for the one who rejects me and does not accept my words; the very words I have spoken will condemn them at the last day."

(John 12:48)

For we must all appear before the judgment seat of Christ, so that each of us may receive what is due us for what the things we have done while in the body, whether good or bad.

(2 Corinthians 5:10)

The words of the wise are like goads, their collected sayings like firmly embedded nails—given by one shepherd. Be warned, my son, of anything in addition to them.

Of making many books there is no end, and much study wearies the body.

Now all has been heard;
    here is the conclusion of the matter:
Fear God and keep his commandments,
    for this is the duty of all mankind.
For God will bring every deed into judgment,
    including every hidden thing,
    whether it is good or evil.

(Ecclesiastes 12:11–14)

"Now what I am commanding you today is not too difficult for you or beyond your reach. It is not up in heaven, so that you have to ask, "Who will ascend into heaven to get it and proclaim it to us so we may obey it?" Nor is it beyond the sea, so that you have to ask, "Who will cross the sea to get it and proclaim it to us so we may obey it?" No, the word is very near you; it is in your mouth and in your heart so you may obey it.

See, I set before you today life and prosperity, death and destruction. For I command you today to love the LORD your God, to walk in obedience to him, and to keep his commands, decrees and laws; then you will live and increase, and the LORD your God will bless you in the land you are entering to possess.

But if your heart turns away and you are not obedient, and if you are drawn away to bow down to other gods and worship them, I declare to you this day that you will certainly be destroyed. You will not live long in the land you are crossing the Jordan to enter and possess.

This day I call the heavens and the earth as witnesses against you that I have set before you life and death, blessings and curses. Now choose life, so that you and your children may live and that you may love the LORD your God, listen to his voice, and hold fast to him." (Deuteronomy 30:11–20)

Some Final Thoughts

This concludes our six studies together. Thank you for allowing me to share my life and thoughts with you. I have done my best to share the mindset, convictions and strategies I have personally used over the years to live a faithful (not perfect) Christian life as a same-sex attracted man. Of course, there is a huge part of me that feels like I have done this quite inadequately as these issues are so complex and emotional and difficult to address. I also realize there are points you may have disagreed with, and am certain you still have questions that remain unanswered, but as I stated at the beginning of this study series, I myself have questions that remain unanswered.

There is, however, something beautiful about living in the midst of mystery, not knowing all of the "why's" and still trusting that as we do this faithfully and courageously (again, not perfectly) for the Jesus, the Lord's love is perfect and his forgiveness and mercy are complete. Please know that as I write this, I am praying for you. I don't know your name, of course, but I know you. I know the struggle, I know the pain, I know the confusion, I know this is not easy, I know you've suffered abuse, but I also know that God loves you, he's not ashamed or embarrassed of you, and I know he wants to use your life to glorify Him, and I know that you CAN live a faithful Christian life as many are doing right now!

Study Six Notes

End Notes

1. M.A. Yarhouse and L.A. Burke. *Sexual Identity: A Guide to Living in the Time Between the Times* (New York: University Press of America, Inc., 2003), 30.

2. Yarhouse and Burke, 30–31.

3. Yarhouse and Burke, 30–31.

4. Wade Meredith, "What Happens to Your Body When You Drink a Coke Right Now?" Healthbolt, 9 October, 2013,   http://dailyhealth-post.com/this-is-what-happens-in-your-body-when-you-drink-a-coke/.

Other Books by Guy Hammond

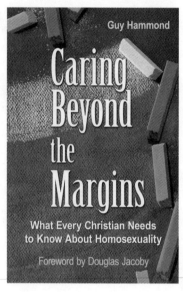

Both available at
www.ipibooks.com

For more information about
Guy Hammond's ministry
go to
www.strengthinweakness.org

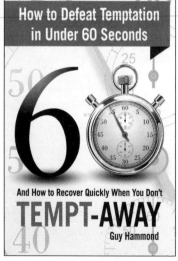